Favorit

by Katie Sharp

HOUGHTON MIFFLIN HARCOURT
School Publishers

PHOTOGRAPHY CREDITS: Cover © Jonathan Nourok/PhotoEdit; 1 © Jupiter Images/Brand X/Alamy; 2 © Jonathan Nourok/PhotoEdit; 3 (tl) © Getty Images, (tr) © EyeWire, (bl) © EyeWire (br) © Brand X Pictures; 4 © Pegaz/Alamy; 5 © Brand X Pictures; 6 © Jupiter Images/Creatas/Alamy; 7 © Jupiter Images/Brand X/Alamy; 8 © Reed Kaestner/Corbis; 9 © Photodisc/Alamy; 10 © Digital Vision/Alamy

Printed in China

ISBN-13: 978-0-547-42711-9
ISBN-10: 0-547-42711-5

6 7 8 0940 18 17 16 15 14 13 12
4500351669

We like bikes.

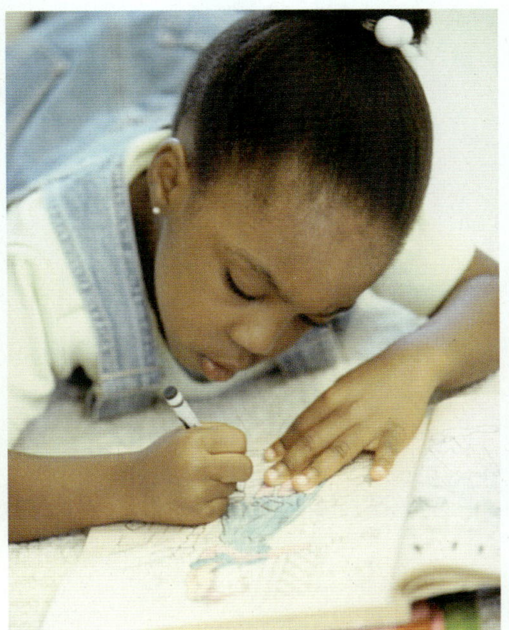

We like crayons.

We like bubbles.
Bubbles can be big.

We like computers.
Computers can help us.

We like trees.

We like books.

We like dogs.

We like baseball.

We can play and play.

We like ice cream.

We can eat it **with** **you**.

Responding

WORDS TO KNOW **Word Builder**

Fill in the missing word in this sentence: We like to _____ baseball.

Talk About It

Text to Self What do you like to do when you play with a friend?

WORDS TO KNOW

and
be
help
play
with
you

TARGET STRATEGY Summarize

Stop to tell important ideas as you read.